KORAH'S DAUGHTER

PREVIOUS BOOKS BY THE SAME AUTHOR

Poetry
Ritual Bath, 1993
Unopened Letters, 1996
The Face in the Window, 2004
Havoc: New & Selected Poems, 2013
Return from Elsewhere, 2014

Translations
Wild Light: Selected Poems of Yona Wallach, 1997
Let the Words: Selected Poems of Yona Wallach, 2006
These Mountains: Selected Poems of Rivka Miriam, 2009

KORAH'S DAUGHTER

LINDA STERN ZISQUIT

All rights reserved. No part of this work covered by the copyright herein may be reproduced or used in any means – graphic, electronic, or mechanical, including copying, recording, taping, or information storage and retrieval systems – without written permission of the publisher.

Printed by imprintdigital
Upton Pyne, Exeter
www.digital.imprint.co.uk

Typesetting and cover design by The Book Typesetters
hello@thebooktypesetters.com
07422 598 168
www.thebooktypesetters.com

Published by Shoestring Press
19 Devonshire Avenue, Beeston, Nottingham, NG9 1BS
(0115) 925 1827
www.shoestringpress.co.uk

First published 2022
© Copyright: Linda Stern Zisquit
© Cover painting: Untitled, oil on canvas, 85 x 64, by Ronit Goldschmidt, 2017
© Author photograph: Avigail Schimmel

The moral right of the author has been asserted.

ISBN 978-1-915553-14-0

ACKNOWLEDGEMENTS

Grateful acknowledgement is extended to the following publications in which these poems first appeared, sometimes in slightly different form:

arc, Beloit Poetry Review, PN Review, Salamander, Salmagundi, Shirim

A sequence of the psalmwork poems was published as a pamphlet *From the Notebooks of Korah's Daughter* by New Walk Editions, Leicester & Nottingham, UK, 2019.

"To Stay the Distance" was printed in my essay "Is It A Test?" in *Nashim: A Journal of Jewish Women's Studies & Gender Issues*, no. 39, Indiana University Press, Fall 2121.

"*...more desirable than gold*" was reprinted in *Tree Lines: 21st Century American Poems*, Grayson Books, West Hartford, CT, 2022.

I want to thank the Hadassah-Brandeis Institute and the Memorial Foundation for Jewish Culture for grants that helped me while working on some of these poems.

My deepest gratitude to Jenny Barber, Nina Bogin and Gabriel Levin for their patience, insight, and close attention to these poems. And to John Lucas, my generous editor.

Thank you to Nick Everett, Lewis Freedman, Diana Lipton, and Alicia Ostriker for reading the poems and for their suggestions.

Thank you also to Peg Boyers, Marie Howe, Mimi Khalvati, Lisa New, Robert Pinsky, Jonathan Price, David Rosenberg, Suzanna Tamminen, Rosanna Warren, Eleanor Wilner and Avivah Zornberg for their inspiration and contributions to my writing life.

A special thank you to Sidra Ezrahi for her companionship and care, and to Donald and our children and grandchildren for their love.

I continue to be grateful to the late Robert Creeley whose abiding friendship still nourishes me.

For Z, who brought me to this mountain

"I remember my music in the night."

Psalm 77

CONTENTS

I
Raft   1
To Stay the Distance   2

II
From the Notebooks of Korah's Daughter   7

III
Psalmwork   23

IV
Sward   45
Nothings   46
Learning My ABCs   51
War Sonata   54

Notes   57

I

RAFT

I was filling a book with writing
about a child's survival, and longing.
As I kept writing the book grew thicker.
What were the pages filled with?
I thought, at least I can write again.
Then I touched his lips and he said
the walls have eyes. He said I wish
but the wish will never be fulfilled.
He said his chest was tightening and
I wish I wish there were some way
to step outside of time. And then
completing the circle he left and I
walked in the other direction. A sea
of words that rather than floating off
and moving out of sight became a raft,
a structure on which we kept our balance,
hardly moving, but for the breeze.

TO STAY THE DISTANCE

What keeps you alive?

I kneel at my child's bed.

What keeps you alive?

*Her fortitude
and the letters from a man.*

Isn't it always like that?

You mean a parallel life?

And the way you find an opening—

*A digression? A detour,
as the doctor called her cancer?*

A road. The porous and the hidden.
What your research was going to be—

Was that it?

In Portugal women hid the rituals
embedded in their aprons, their seasonings:
shards of ancient melody
like amulets wrapped in swathing
became the only remnant.

*There is another lost thread,
a maze of—*

No, it is a clear narrative line
to the missing—

*I wanted to salvage some conversation
in their tangled
and desperate
slide.*

Was it a mountain or a pit that trapped them?

Both.

*A couple in Japan had been arguing
then came the wind, earth broke beneath them
he was pinned from the neck down under the rocks
she was motionless but for her mouth
promising a future if they survived the quake
their voices almost mute from the dust and weight.*

And yet hers was heard.

*At least I think
that's what happened—*

They were spotted
by a helicopter

*and slowly limb by limb
lifted.*

Life returned.

Unlike the Polish couple among the lost—

A father and daughter
hiding in a pit

*Their voices muted not by the concrete or wood of their secret cellar
but by the force of laughter and forgetting that permits
even the most outrageous acts to be endured.
Together they stood.*

How did they eat or urinate or exercise?

How did they stay there in complete silence
till the sounds of the living defeated them?

How do you go on living?

I told you I follow my child's lead
humbled by our luck in the past
strengthened by a man's attention
as if my words held meaning.

Isn't that it, to tell the truth—
so your words hold meaning?

We speak of passion
responsibility
end
of all that has held me in its grip—

Because to repeat the past
with its excesses
is not to honour the other path—

The railing I hold on to
not to fall
or fail

the test—

Is it a test, and if so which one?

To stay the distance
To keep the hidden intact

and the bold undiminished sun

and the Palestine sunbird in her nest
near my kitchen window.

II

FROM THE NOTEBOOKS OF KORAH'S DAUGHTER

How did I walk away unscathed as the rest of my family tumbled into the earth's chasm: my father leading them all in blue all equal all artful, my brothers hanging onto roots and loose rock till their voices could no longer be discerned, their plaintive notes rising from the highest ledge like fire fastened to a mast? I put my ear to the crust as it was closing over them, tapped my fingers to the beat as if to answer them. Let my flaws become fluid in these lines and my split allegiance keep me riveted to the point between as I wander in a future riddled with questions. Listen: is it the sons of my father or a bird of desire who sings?

Or did I follow them down into the pit, my eyes wide open, and come back like Isaac blinded by the angel's tears?

Or was it a dream—a nightmare or fantasy?

If I was there and couldn't keep them from falling why do I not remember their astonished faces or the flame?

I was untouched. I survive. I cannot stop the tremors. Is that the earth, the after-shock? Or my body, after death, revived?

How can I accept a god who punishes the unruly with such carnage, cleaving the ground beneath them, opening the earth's mouth and swallowing them alive?

I thought I was coming home to rest. I am restless. I have been looking for my shepherd. Who is hidden. My father is buried in the rubble. And my mother, why didn't she stop him?

I carry a small charm in my pocket, a smooth sculpted relief of a woman, an angel, a virgin – or is she a victim? Like my distant cousin warm in the bed of a foreigner killed by her brothers. Where was her father to stop them? Or the girl in the field whose cries are not heard. Where is her father to protect her? Or the dutiful daughter of the reckless judge? or the one punished with rape and degradation for her father's martyrdom? Who speaks for them?

He has hidden His face; He will never see

Wherever I look, there you were meant
to be. In villages and towns, on the road
to the station, there you must be,
your shadow over everything. The acts
called evil are witnessed. But where
are the eyes and ears that will verify
these things? Like the perpetrator you
hide. The lion. The mocker. Is that
the work of a god, to join the pack
of those who lurk unseen?
On the agitated lane I meet friends,
comfort a child who is pressed
with the weight of your hiddenness,
with the moving force of war and
prophecy. With the inability to take a
breath amid the smoke, to breathe
as your presence nears, to recognize it.

We are daughters of men whose actions must mark us.

What is inherited? From where this desire to create art out of restlessness? Daughter of a willful man, do I learn to hold my tongue? No, I give voice to her and her and her.

Wasn't my father's crime an attempt to retrieve what was rightfully his? Or simply to stop the stutterer from winning him over and toppling his silence with speech?

Korah means bald; he sealed all desire inside and would not speak; the earth became barren, without a strand of grass.

My father challenged the hierarchy of power. He questioned the source of its elite holiness.

Korah closed his mouth to the envied leader who fell on his face in grief. Am I the bearer of his transgression? I am scarred and freed by my father's violent death. Is my ongoing experience of eros a way of embracing him, or erasing him?

I alone of my family survived. I look at worlds from outside and in, above and below. I enter the story by speaking.

Traces of mats and vendors and broken wells. Scorched nettles and fig trees and caper plants.

What do I learn from my father's story, his punishment, his cool hands and blocked ears, his mouth full of stones? Enough and too much. Borders and limits and walls and cracks.

Did it require the disappearance of all I depended on – mother, father, brothers - before I could walk and talk on my own? Or was it simply then clear, what was mine, this song – the babble of a newborn, the timbre of a solitary bird suddenly melded with all I had heard and learned from the elders, distilling out and keeping in, my ears awash with sounds of the sands and the trickle of water on the rock face.

Silence closes the heart, opens the wound. The movement of eros enables life. If we don't keep talking, the movement stops, the earth cleaves beneath us.

I hear my brothers' chorus through a crack of light.

Where am I going and who will I be at the end? I go to the little words that spring from rupture (rapture)

freed of impediments (not everything needs to be told)

to the edge of an abyss: precipice, witness, test, law, ecstasy

(an immense freedom)

At night one may weep, but joy comes in the morning

As though a sun rose inside us. Or
pulling ourselves up from the pit into light.
A scribe expresses desire, but displaced.
In stone. Or the beaten metal of a sunken
craft. It is through objects he can speak
of memory charged with forgetfulness.
Like a spirit-sailor tossed between
anchor and gale, torn between beauty
and the strict vows of a nazirite. To him
I embody division, our conversation
limned with coded hints of intimacy.
At night I weep, I try to sleep. The way
the sea returns to shore, and expectations
rise in waves, carrying me out.

I don't remember writing any of this. Was it in a trance, after my father's fall, under a sorcerer's spell?

...in Your light we see light

We eat and drink and are sated.
The house abounds in your feast.
Is it hubris to speak of a
light-filled house?
A mother chants the word
summons
to see what is called to her:
a song she hums as shadows
flicker on a child's face.
You let us drink
from your spring
to quench our thirst,
brighten us with your gift.
The hole is dark and deep:
a silence of cries,
a barren hollow. Lift us
till we can bear your light.

Why do I tell this story, when did it happen, and where, in the desert camp or outside near a small village teahouse?

Do I carry my father's grave (an earthquake) inside me?

I must go back to living in my body. Summer ended quickly.

Chronicler of rebellion and return, Receiver of time lost and found, Surveyor of envy and lack: maybe it was for this purpose I survived, to tell a story of trauma, of misplaced passion and memory bent by attachments. Like a plough overturning the fecund past, reopening the earth's wound till new soil with its dark moisture and fragrant life erupts at my feet.

III

PSALMWORK

...like a tree planted by rivers of water

Not to think moving to another
room will open the pores or seal
the sorrow. It seeps in because
you are the keeper who lets it in.
No door wide open or shut would have
let this happen. Clear from the start:
a tree, *yielding its fruit in season.*
At the bottom of steps a garden grows.
I could go outside and drink in
the green. For now I must keep myself
fixed to this chair, this text. Yesterday
they dug deep, cut the hole
clean to the root, not a cell left
to fester or seek an unseen crack,
then closed the wound to heal,
nothing withered. By chance today
I draw an image of before – the hair,
the mouth, the brow: a girl
emerging from the stream, urgent
yet uncertain, her fullness
smiling out at me.

Why do nations rage and people think only of vanities

Anxious to see him, how could it be otherwise!
Will he come from behind and scare off
the light? Or from in front where lifting my
face the light of his will shine? Is that his
whistle, or another's? Would I recognize
his step? We speak of a poet's tears
after years away from home: the island,
the quiet sea, the sun. Why exiled? For songs
in a foreign tongue! And why did I embrace him
on the street just as the elder walked by?
Was it in order to be banished, never to
see him again? The man in the long black robe
could not have seen us and smiled as he passed.
Still I took an oath not to endanger him again.
Not to allow the open windows and waiting faces
to condemn. If I leave of my own volition
I avoid the vanity and rage, the fiction of wisdom.

I lie down and sleep and wake

Even as I lie to your face. Even as I
pursue the wrong path. Blot out
my mistakes and nothing remains:
gaps and stolen music from between
the two pear trees. Even there
the fruit falls. Too soon it ripens
and I must gather the rotten,
the pungent, the worm-infested.
Yet this troubled sleep is balm
because it takes me and holds me
and does not question what I did
in daylight, now erased. What is
sleep? Sustain me. I no longer promise
to be good. And still sleep comes.
Or vow to be clean. No. The white
linen soiled, my sweat where flesh
desires more. I don't ask for
stillness or for stone, chiselled as
the stoic, the monk, the penitent.
Only for soft earth, its throbbing
mouth, fresh grass with its wetness,
the heart listening, awake now, alone.

For the musician on stringed instruments, answer when I call

We are hanging by a thread.
Rumours of more dead, rumours that
pass like a measure of song whispered
in ears: "dead, our sons are dead."
How will I write the next line
or go out on a summer day to sing?
If you hear when I call to you why
don't you answer? It is demeaning
to think we are bound to a fate
that keeps taking our young.
Let them run with their mates
for two months to the hills,
to dance and lament the kisses
ungiven, like Yiftah's daughter
fulfilling a father's reckless vow,
as if this were the promise
that puts gladness in our hearts.

With an eight-stringed harp. In the grave who can give thanks?

I will try with my fingers to pluck
the chords to please you. Though I
have never been fully turned or
tuned to your mercy. As the demon
slips into my veins *I cause my bed
to swim*, out of desire for him,
not you. And not in grief, but
longing. It is my instrument,
the body's heat. And the wooden
bridge across which my bow plays
is taut. Still I am one of the lost,
my bones frightened not by a spear
or a soldier's bleeding arm
but in fear of nothing but this
pulsing lyre. With an eight-
stringed lark the skies explode.
With an eight-stringed heart
the body tenses and knows.
Keep me from silencing my song.

What is man, that You keep him in mind

How easily we fall. The boy. The man.
The doomed daughter liberated
by death from the moon and stars
that you have pinned in place.
How is it they remain fixed
and you have let the boy loose,
the man unhinged from his home,
a stray jackal roaming the hills,
howling? What is the mind
in which you keep us unarmed
against your cosmos? No belief or creed
is strong enough to cry out: more.
Not even your name over the earth.

You have destroyed their cities; the memory of them is gone

Only names if we give them names
will call back what happened.
Even in our tongue, though they
spoke another. Even if *graves
of desire* are left open, the spoils
spread around, ravaged
as Tyre. Even if we recount
the journey from the death of their
first-born to Moab, to Canaan,
even if we track their steps
with a line across their land and
ours, it is only by naming them
that we can be forgiven, or forgive
ourselves who traverse the same route
spotted with nettles and revenge.

How can you say to my soul, flee as a bird to your mountain?

Trembling in our cage of fear, our fingers too weak
to grip the bars: we are in the care of careless men.
A girl cries from an underground tunnel, not the hole

of bitumen and pitch, but a buried light that is poetry.
A man whistles in the orchard. It took him
hours to arrive from Beit Hanina, 'House of Pity.'

He offers a hand amid the bulbul's noisy song as if
to mark a meeting ground. Her voice carries through
a faint line, reaches me with its cry like a small bird's.

How long must I devise plans in my soul, have sorrow in my heart all day?

My disordered mind turns in two
directions when I speak these words:
toward skies filled with the babble
of baby sparrows mimicking their
parents, testing and sounding
till they emit a call of their own;

and toward Sheol where I cannot
hear a wing's whir, now that he
who leaves is silent: as he crosses
the universe no echo over the earth,
as I recall his tremor and know
in his throat are movements
and in his chest a fluttering.

…who has counseled me, even on nights when my thoughts are tortured

Who has brought me to this mountain
surrounded by trees, looking out
on Lebanon after a day of intense
heat, serene as the stretch of grass
before the sanctuary walls? We climbed
ramparts, walked between pillars
and poles to a dusty shrine
within the pine-tree hedge of a village.
I have come to this refuge under
the good auspices of some god.
A soldier captured, two more dead.
My own battle goes on within.
He who has counseled me at night –
even when my thoughts are
tortured, when longing is more than
I can bear – has brought me here.

*Guard me like the pupil of an eye; hide me in the shadow of
Your wings*

Wrens rehearse a local song, perch
in acacia native to this landscape.
There are patterns, chants
the birds learn before they claim
a call of their clan. I have unlearned
and discarded the elders' melody.
What I call seamless is the movement
from meeting him on a mountainside
and going home alone, the contour
of his body imprinted on my bare skin
that is never allowed to touch his.
Borders and wholeness are his
territory. Mine is lawless, broken.
Guard me like the pupil of an eye,
keep me within distance of sight, so
the shadow over my footsteps is called God.

He brought me out into open space; He rescued me because He delighted in me

We walked in the woods at dawn toward
an ancient red-bark tree when a pig-like
dog appeared on the path. It kept a few
paces behind as if assigned to us.
Once we cleared the rusty gate it took
the lead. Whenever we slowed down
because of loose rocks it went slower too,
entangling with our legs,
then racing ahead. Suddenly it stopped,
snarled and lunged at a thick snake
twisting and hissing from the branch above.
We spun round and ran, praying
it would show up breathless at our feet,
unsightly saviour, angel of flight!
Entangled in the underbrush, how
do I sing of safety when I ache
to escape its wing? Like the ecstatic ones
who turned aside from your mountain
courting danger and mistake, I follow
every arrow leading me astray: where
is the hiss, the snarl to save me again?

...more desirable than gold

He spoke after love of honey.
The sun that shone behind him
blazed around us
though we were in shadow.
A bee dozed by.
If there is suffering there is also memory.
I cannot forget the moment of his breath
or the light around his face,
a tree rustling,
pebbles stirring beneath us.
He said tomorrow and meant yesterday.
Gold becomes dim in the eyes
of the tired, the fire ceases to rage.
There is no utterance, there are no words
whose sound goes unheard:
speech of tree and whisper of stone.
Only the sun still burns
with a glint of his gaze.

May He remember all your offerings. And accept your burnt sacrifice.

But nothing counts if we call it
victory. To be thankful is not enough
after war's obscenity: the feasts and
banners and rites and horns and drums
and shouts of joy. We grow dull,
callous with relief, hardened to other
cries in the stony field. Or we wake,
bend close to the ground, ear
to the grieving sand, heart humbled.

That I use the language of psalms
to sing of love, of honey in our mouths,
of his gold-rimmed face, is another
sacrilege. It is not enough to write
these words. Like the delicate spring
blossoms of the amaryllis I must
tough it out all summer, refrain from
easing away in the scent of his
robe. Not to forget your offering.

On Ayelet Hashahar. Gazelle of the Dawn

The cows and bulls surround me as we
hike up the hill to the temple ruins.
They follow me, strong bulls of Bashan
encircle me. *They open their mouths
wide at me, like ravenous roaring lions.*
Dogs snarl. Two roosters in a tree
at Bir'am tell of my wrongdoing. They
peck and stare as I count all my bones.
*I have so many coverings, they divide
my garments among them and cast lots
for my clothing.* The miraculous hand
of their god manipulates my regret.
Night brings no rest, I rub hyssop
for sleep, trace dogs and bulls and lions
retreating, fathom all the forms of
foreign love till I can taste the seed
of home, till my tongue does not cleave.

Who may stand in His holy place? He who has clean hands and a pure heart

I cleared the hours of the afternoon
to meet him in a cool tent. I washed
my body till it shone. I studied a treatise
to set the words of the wise on my tongue
before speaking with him. And he has
distanced himself from vanity and tired
of deception. He has a fortress to protect
from outside and in. He may stand
in the holy place with clean hands now.
I trip as I enter. Still it is half-open
to me, a door I could have closed
when first he appeared. Who can say
a heart is pure, pulsing its lonely poem?

Malicious witnesses rise up; they ask of me things I do not know

Set judges at the gate, it is said,
and always at least two witnesses.
No crime exists if unseen:
things I do not know.
Like my secret in the field
where no witness came.
No one demands of me
justice or payment.
Only one whisper rises up
facing *Elul*, month of questions,
asking why did he lead me there
and why did I follow.
No one can prove I did not go
of my own will. No one can say
he kissed me or undid me
so I could not return from there
the same. Malicious witnesses
rise up within me. They propose
it was a crime I committed,
malicious witnesses who ask of me
things I do not know: tender as
the tissue of sex, tender as his tongue,
tender as the trap where we lay.

What troubles you, sea, that you flee?

Is there a plan we cannot fathom?
The shawl she wore to veil her face
allowed the prudent man to know her.
The coat the brothers stained to hide their deed
betrayed their blood-tie to him.
The cloak she pulled from the servant's
beautiful back when he refused her and fled
remained in her hand as proof
of self-deception. We hide our tears
to protect a lie of recognition.
Recognize this! And a father understands
his beloved boy is torn apart
by a beast of his own conjuring.
We are a moon tied to radiance
by a thread, we turn back and wait
to be thrust out, in turn, like the tide.

Rescue me

Falling snow covers the ground,
pressing down the branches, brightening
the night. We give thanks
for her recovery, your white clarity
around us, protecting us.
Yesterday I met him at a well.
We spoke across the deep, never touching.
Rabbit in one language
could mean hunt or eat or brown
in translation. Asaph as a feminine
composer. Word-play before the second
sleep. These are the things we spoke of.
Not the tug and pull or even the music
that played silently between
us. Like a sudden snowfall at dusk.

Place a guard at my mouth; watch over the door to my lips.

These words I whisper are prohibited,
our promises silenced like bones
at the mouth of a grave.

IV

SWARD

You come to a clearing
like the knoll before the ancient temple
in Bar'am
a village emptied of its
inhabitants
still waiting to return.
You find a grassy open landing
and understand that
all the waiting
can only be held inside
so long.
It reaches a crescendo
like the hornblast rising
or the bell tower
tolling
till everything must fall
or break
or return to its source:
the memory
of how the house smelled
when they lived within its walls
and how the gravel underfoot
sounded as they went up the path
without a worry or threat
in mind,
even the day before.
That is the reality of your longing.
You come to a sward
before the ruins
carrying this hope so long
that you can put it down
on the green
and leave
without ever knowing
its smell
or sound.

NOTHINGS

> Ethereal things may at least be thus real, divided under three heads—Things real, things semi-real—and nothings… Nothings… are made great and dignified by an ardent pursuit.
> – John Keats, letter to Benjamin Bailey, 13 March 1818

*

It is never what you say it is
not the caffeine
or the sleeplessness
or the traffic
or the pile of clothes
you threw on the floor
or the lost key
or the list of chores
it is never the obvious
or the spoken
or the hidden revealed
it is somewhere else
buried yet acknowledged
by the skin
trampled on when you
aren't looking
but it is there
the wing that once
could fly
now folded into
the narrowest
crevice of
the heart where
the rock
and the pasture
and the voice are found

*

You must put it aside
what encompassed you

and filled you
must be removed
cut away
peeled off
scraped out
not a trace of it
can remain inside
or out
it must be
excised
from the
depths
and flung as far
as the arm can throw
and there can be
nothing of it left
not a mote of dust
from its afternoon light
or a spectre of sun
or a rim of moon
none of it
none of it lasts
none of it
can last
at last

    *

You wait
for a word
that does not come
you believe it is
on its way
but really
it is waiting for
you to stop
waiting
for it to proceed
on its way

you cannot
forget the sound
of its arrival
like the mail
that would drop
into the vestibule
at Christmastime
several times
a day
and all you want
is to hear that sound
of mail dropping
of someone writing
to answer your
letter
that you sent
from your heart
but instead
you receive
silence
because that is the
best teacher
the one who
makes it clear
you will hear
nothing
no sound
in the empty
box
no message
in the dark
night
no response

*

You wake at 4
to the darkness
of a dream

you go through
the path of forest
and stones
till you find
an opening
there you proceed
and walk
till you come
to a gate
that was not
open before
and you reach
out your hand
that is not
warm or wet
and it gently
moves the
metal door
that leads
to another
gate and you
behold
what you
chose to
deny
when it was
unseen
the need to
enter
and to live
in the place
you have
built
and to
care
for the walls
and roof
as if they
could break

or dissolve
at the breath
of you

LEARNING MY ABCs
[a loose adaption in response to Psalm no. 119 which follows an alphabetical pattern.]

After all there is law and there is deviance.

And those who walk between are careful to keep their eyes open.

Anyone will tell you blindness can sharpen one's vision.

A beggar approached my car at a red light and I asked him to hand me the scarf that was caught in the door.

As if I were the one in need I thanked him and forgot to put something in his hand.

Attending to my own suffering I have lost the art of bending in time to the unexpected.

Another lack becomes apparent when unkind words leak out.

Before the evening comes I must recite these lines.

Because there is a pattern to the day and night and light goes before I am done.

Borrow from my man's generous heart that brings comfort when I have offended him.

Candles will be lit in honour of the coming holiday.

Cancer wracked our daughter's body and now she is clean of it.

Care for her. Carry her on your wings, clandestine angel of healing and contemplation.

Can these eyes see wonderful things from your Law?

Desire opened my eyes to strange and unforgettable shame.

Dawn will greet me after sleep.

Every afternoon in June and then July my heart turned to another and the moments became two narrow mountains and a sliver of sky.

Enough time has passed so that what was earth is dust and what was sky is cloud and what we held is confined to the word, encounter.

Elements of the past remain within my body's structure and like a magnet it pulls and like a vice it tightens.

Forget the secret conversation and the festive harmonics.

Follow the small vowels that seem to lead nowhere.

Give voice to what my hands cannot hold and my heart cannot keep for its own.

How I rushed to avoid its message how I could have missed its gracious word.

Heal the sleeplessness with thanks. At midnight I bend my body into a cradle of sufficient warmth.

It was the warp and weft of our correspondence that bound us and separated us like the stamp pressed to an envelope and then sent off into its unresolved orbit.

Inferior hearts would say it ended with parting.

I cannot forget the kisses of his mouth. The love fixed in my body like a barbed wire.

June brought longing and sickness.

July came with its heat.

Kind is the man who keeps me safe.

Keepsake is my body remembering.

Look! the way is lit with darkness.

Let me see wholeness in our human embrace.

Marked by what was and its bounty of love.

My soul left me when he spoke.

Nearly swept into the stream.

Old man buried without seeing his older son, older son buried without speaking to his brother, masters of the rational, sad musicians of history and hoarding.

Pleasure in the night warmth and covering as the wind howls and the trees shake.

Quince. Persimmon. Oyster mushrooms. Chestnuts. Jerusalem artichokes. I turn my ear to their music.

Rain falls all night and the roof holds.

Sign of honest and upright intention. Yet if the tool I use to chop wood flies off and hits another, who is responsible? A city of refuge protects the one whose axe is broken.

Scared of the wishbone's latent power I took it into my own hands and the stronger side fell to my right.

Testimony. Place a hand under the thigh. Or the testicles. Where word and want are synonymous. Witness and truth. He has seen me borrow and lie. He has heard my divided step.

Terror in the supermarket and in the newsroom. Terror in the café when I hear a plate drop.

Unhinged as a cable spinning or a dancer stumbling at the onset of paralysis and pain

Untethered I leave and return. He digs wells and lifts stones.

WAR SONATA

It was unlike anything else.

Using the past tense must refer to music that cannot stay but is all movement

or passion that doesn't lie, as Marina Tsvetaeva said, but also doesn't last.

Orpheus agreed to the condition not to speak to his love or turn around to be sure her soundless footfalls followed him.

Isn't it something to agree to such conditions when the music continues and the heart strings do not rest?

I agreed not to speak.

But that was after the first movement. Already conditioned to his notes our chords the incredible harmony—

What was it? a change of rhythm, too long a pause after the crest, a rippling that could not return to its whirling center?

I agreed even then

because I refused to let the song end. A false attenuated finale? Or like the head on the water that keeps singing its grief, I could not unlearn the song.

In the first moments, there were no words, only notes made of holes.

On the river, as if a boat kept us afloat, I repeated measures of an earlier rapture. I turned to him and tried to touch his flesh. And like some god who repels because of a higher law, he pushed me away.

As if one could enter the underworld and speak the language of innocence, I repeated my error. I lost him again. And again.

That was the scenario until the evening performance of Prokofiev's Sonata in B-flat major Opus 83 performed by Sara Daneshpour.

Andante dolce.

I wanted to sleep.

Prokofiev's wasn't the music I wanted to hear.

Its dissonant lyrics. Its sweetness. Its lies.

It kept waking me.

Andante sognando. Slow and dreamy.

Girls in the row in front kept pressing the keys of their cell phones, lighting the dark, drawing my eyes, but they didn't interrupt the hush as she played.

She wore a silver shimmering sheath. Suddenly her hair moved in one flash as she swayed

vivace

octaves brutal
and
divine

1939

Alive!

It was then without thought my body reconstructed

something in me started to rise

a solo symphony

primordial flame, forgotten promise, skirmishes, bruises, sand thrown in my face

a billowy spray, a shield. The music covered me.

NOTES

Korah's daughter is the imagined daughter of the biblical Korah who rebelled against his cousins Moses and Aaron and who, together with his sons and followers, was swallowed up by the earth [Numbers 16: 1–33]. According to legend, Korah's sons repented and became psalmists, singers on the highest rung of the underworld [Numbers 26:10]. No daughter of Korah appears in the traditional sources.

from Midrash Tehillim:

The verse *But his delight is in the law of the Lord* (Ps. 1:2) applies to the sons of Korah, who composed a Psalm, saying: Are we still bound to honour our father [or] ought we to accord honour to Moses our teacher? Thereupon they decided in favour of honouring Moses.

And he shall be like a tree planted by the rivers of water (Ps. 1:1). This verse, too, applies to the sons of Korah. After Korah and his company were swallowed up, Korah's sons remained standing like a boat's mast, as it is said, *They remained like a mast* (Num. 26:10). Rabbi said, "All the area around them was rent, but the ground they stood upon was not rent." R. Samuel bar Nahman explained that the three sons of Korah were not standing together in one place, but that each was by himself, so that after the earth was rent they stood like three pillars. Accordingly, in the popular saying, "On what does the earth stand? On three pillars," the three are said by some to refer to Abraham, Isaac, and Jacob, by others to Hananiah, Mishael, and Azariah, and by still others to the three sons of Korah.

The English translations from the Bible are based on the *JPS Hebrew-English Tanakh*, the *New American Standard Bible*, the *King James Version,* and Machom Mamre's *Hebrew-English Bible.*

The 'psalmwork' poems are associative responses to the *Book of Psalms*. In their essence psalms are outcries, and reciting psalms is a traditional Jewish method of crying out to God in times of individual and communal crisis.

Isaac (p. 7): son of Abraham, father of Jacob. In one midrash as Abraham is about to sacrifice Isaac bound on the altar, the angels are weeping. Their tears fall into Isaac's wide-open eyes, causing his later blindness from this traumatic near-death experience.

The girl in the field (p. 10) "For he found her in the field; the betrothed damsel cried, and there was none to save her." [Deuteronomy 22:27]

nazirite: (p. 16) from *nazar* (Hebrew) literally, to separate; a nazirite is an ascetic who abstains from alcohol, does not cut his hair and is devoted to the service of God.

"a poet" (p. 24): possibly refers to Elisha ben Abuya a Talmudic period rabbi and scholar who adopted a worldview considered heretical by the religious sages of his time; they continued to cite his brilliant teaching by referring to him as "Acher" meaning "other." One theory about time in the Bible is that "there is no early and no late;" therefore Korah's daughter of biblical time may have had knowledge of the future Elisha ben Abuya who would appeal to her as a rebellious poet. Or it may refer to Ovid the Roman poet exiled to Tomis who yearned for his homeland.

Yiftah of Gilad (p. 26) appears in the Book of Judges. He was a judge who led the Israelites in battle against Ammon and, after defeating the Ammonites, fulfilled a frivolous oath to sacrifice his daughter [Judges 11: 30–40].

"graves of desire": (p. 29) in Numbers 11:34 "And the name of that place was called *Kibroth-hataavah*, because there they buried the people that lusted."

Sheol: (p. 31) underworld

speech of tree and whisper of stone (p. 35) from an Ugaritic epic [*Ancient Near Eastern Texts Relating to the Old Testament* as cited in the *Jewish Study Bible*, Oxford University Press, 1999, p. 1303]; according to the same source, an alternative rendering of "their sound is not heard" means that the celestial bodies "speak" soundlessly; they convey their message simply by being.

Elul: (p. 39) Hebrew month before the Days of Awe

shawl, coat, cloak (p. 40) refer to the stories of Tamar and Yehuda [Genesis 38: 14], Joseph's brothers [Genesis 37: 31–32] and Potiphar's wife [Genesis 39: 12–14] who each used a piece of clothing for deception.

beast of his own conjuring (p. 40) refers to Jacob's state of mind when he sees the bloody coat and, knowing it is his son Joseph's, says "an evil beast has devoured him, without doubt he is torn to pieces" טָרֹף טֹרַף [Genesis 37: 33]. Some interpretations examine Jacob's unconscious fears and sense of guilt and responsibility for Joseph's fate.

Learning My ABCs (pp. 51–53) "…the kisses of your mouth" *Song of Songs*: 1.2

"Love was fixed in her body like a barbed arrow" Ovid, Metamorphoses, Book III, l. 395 and Ted Hughes' "Echo and Narcissus" *Tales from Ovid:*, p. 77

"My soul left me when he spoke" *Song of Songs*: 5.6